This book is all about me .

_____

(name)

and

SOCCER!

I am _____ years old
and live in

_____
(city and state)

I am an awesome player
for the

_____
(team name)

Here I am ready to play!

(attach photo)

My coach is

_____.

(attach photo or draw a picture)

My team practices really hard every _____

from _____ to _____.

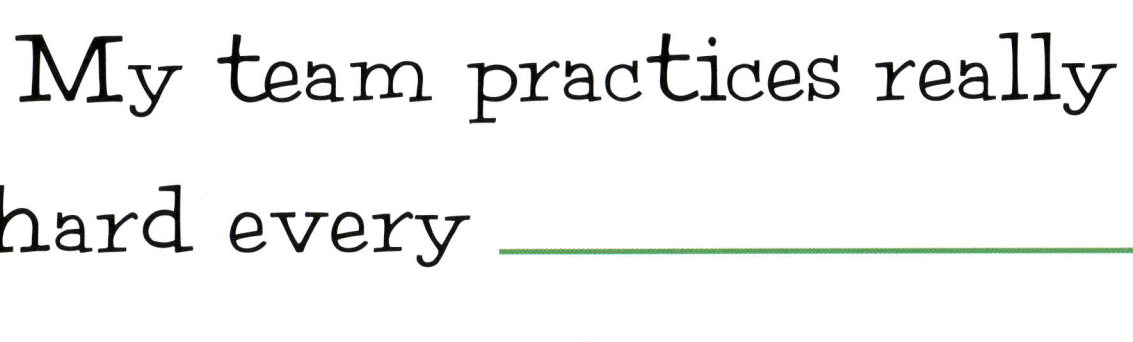

_____ takes me to practice. The hardest thing we do at practice is _____

_____.

My favorite position to play is

_____

because _____

_____.

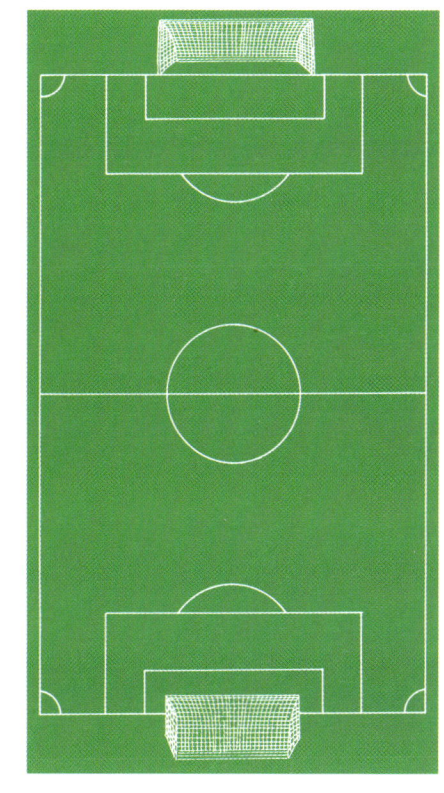

We play our games on

_____

and I like it when

_____

comes to watch! After a
game, my friends and I like
to _____

  _____

 _____.

My teammates are

(color to look like your uniform)

My best friend on the team is _____!

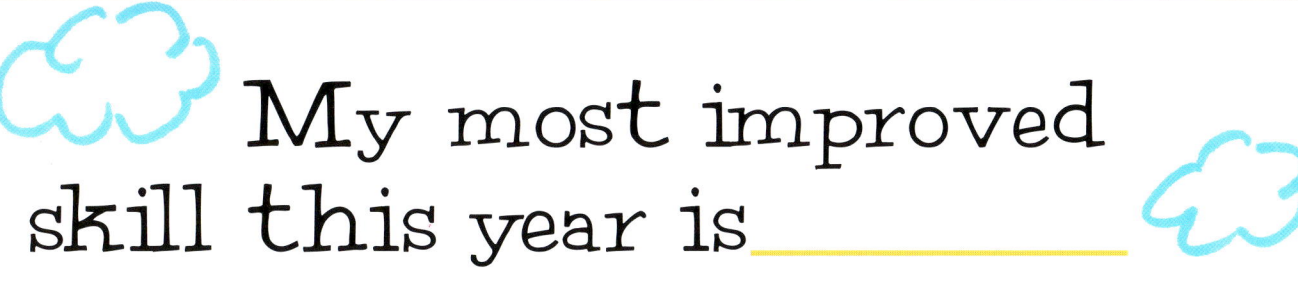

My most improved skill this year is _____

_____.

Next year, I want to be able to _____

_____.

I play soccer
because _____

_____

_____

_____

_____

_____

We finished
our season
with _____ wins!

The toughest team we
played was _____.

We celebrated the end
of the season _____

_____

_____ !

Autographs
& PHOTOS